Digging Canadian Dinosaurs

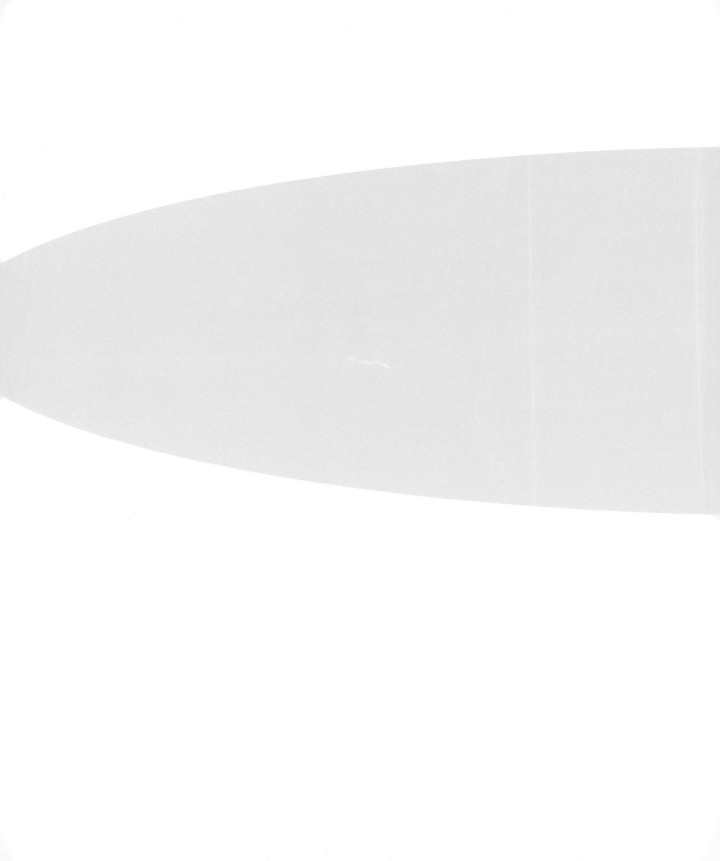

Digging Canadian Dinosaurs

Text by Rebecca L. Grambo

Illustrations by Dianna Bonder

WALRUS
BOOKS

Edited by Elizabeth McLean
Cover and interior design by Tanya Lloyd Kyi

Printed and bound in Canada.

NATIONAL LIBRARY OF CANADA CATALOGUING IN PUBLICATION DATA
Grambo, Rebecca, 1963–
    Digging Canadian dinosaurs / Rebecca L. Grambo ; illustrated by
    Dianna Bonder

    ISBN 1-55285-395-0

    1. Dinosaurs—Canada—Juvenile literature. 2. Paleontology—
    Juvenile literature. I. Bonder, Dianna, 1970– II. Title.

QE861.5.G73 2004   J567.9'0971   C2004-900364-X

The publisher acknowledges the support of the Canada Council and
the Cultural Services Branch of the Government of British Columbia
in making this publication possible. We acknowledge the financial
support of the Government of Canada through the Book Publishing
Industry Development Program for our publishing activities.

Contents

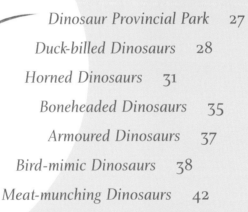

Dinosaur Times

Dinosaurs lived a long time ago—so long it can be hard to imagine that much time and how it fits into our scale of things. Paleontologists (pale-ee-on-TAHL-uh-jists), people who study ancient life, break up some of that huge stretch of time into three unequal sections called eras. The Paleozoic ("ancient life") era, Mesozoic ("middle life") era, and Cenozoic ("recent life") era each span hundreds of millions of years. Dinosaurs lived during the Mesozoic era (250–65 million years ago), which is broken down into three periods: the Triassic (250–203 million years ago), Jurassic (203–135 million years ago), and Cretaceous (135–65 million years ago). Beginning 230 million years ago, many different kinds of dinosaurs evolved and went extinct. But as a group, they dominated the land until 65 million years ago.

What were dinosaurs? Not all big, dead animals qualify. An animal's skeleton must have the right characteristics. That is why flying reptiles such as pteranodons and swimming reptiles such as plesiosaurs are not dinosaurs even though they lived during dinosaur times. Not all dinosaurs were huge, either. Some were about the size of chickens. Speaking of chickens, you may have eaten fried dinosaur: most paleontologists now believe that birds are dinosaur descendants.

Scientists divide the history of life on Earth into three large segments called eras. Shown left to right, they are the Paleozoic ("ancient life") era, Mesozoic ("middle life") era, and Cenozoic ("recent life") era.

Paleontologists sort dinosaurs into two groups based on the structure of their hip bones. Ornithischian (or-nih-THIS-kee-an) dinosaurs have birdlike hips. Saurischian (sore-IS-kee-an) dinosaurs have hips resembling those of lizards. All of the ornithischians were plant-eaters, or herbivores (HER-bih-vorz). The saurischians include some of the giant herbivores and all of the meat-eating carnivores (KAR-nih-vorz).

Look at your arm and imagine that life on Earth began at your shoulder. Dinosaurs appeared at your elbow and all but the birds vanished at your wrist. What about humans? Our time on the planet fits into the tips of your fingernails!

People have only been studying dinosaurs for about 150 years. At first, we imagined them as slow-moving, sluggish creatures. Fossils have since shown us that some dinosaurs could run faster than we can. Others may have migrated vast distances in huge herds. Who knows what new discoveries will reveal?

People flock to dinosaur exhibits in museums and to movies that show how they might have lived. What makes animals that lived millions of years ago so irresistible today? Dinosaurs look like weird beasts from some science fiction tale. But they were real animals that lived on the same planet we do. During their 160-million-year reign, they lived all over Earth and their bones have been found on every continent. Some of the most amazing dinosaurs lived in what is now Canada. Scientists are working to uncover their stories and share them with us.

Rock Stars

The story of dinosaurs is written in stone. How do you get from a walking, eating animal to bones in rocks? We can imagine the process for a dinosaur bone. For a bone to become a fossil, the dinosaur must be buried quickly and gently once it dies. This keeps it from rotting and stops scavengers from pulling the body apart. Many of the best fossils come from rocks that formed in water. Imagine our dead dinosaur sinking in water to a soft bottom and slowly being covered with fine mud.

Now our mud-encased dinosaur has to stay buried long enough for minerals carried by groundwater to replace the material of the bones. Once that happens, our bone is a fossil. The minerals make the fossil heavier and harder than the original bone.

Fossils can form in other ways, too. If an animal dies in a very dry place, the body may dry out quickly and not rot. Paleontologists have found dinosaurs that appear to have died and been buried during a desert sandstorm. Or if an animal somehow falls into a tar pit or peat bog, its body can be preserved by chemicals and eventually fossilized.

Many traces of once living things, such as teeth, leaves, feathers, wood, and animal tracks, can appear in rocks as fossils. Paleontologists even unearth pieces of fossilized droppings (feces) called coprolites (KOH-proh-lites). Dinosaur coprolites as big as 40 centimetres (16 inches) across have been found!

Of course, unless a fossil comes to the surface, no one will ever see it. And if someone does not find a fossil soon enough after it emerges from the rock, wind and rain will wear it away into dust. There will be no evidence that it ever existed.

The fossils paleontologists find are like snapshots of the history of life on Earth, taken when conditions were just right to preserve the information. Most of the plants and animals that have lived on our planet have left no record behind. That is why the fossils that we do have are so important.

The process that turned a dinosaur into a fossil required conditions that were just right from the time the animal died until minerals replaced its bones. At that point, the fossils could have stayed buried or come to the surface and eroded away without being found. Without fossils to tell us their stories, we would not have known that dinosaurs ever existed.

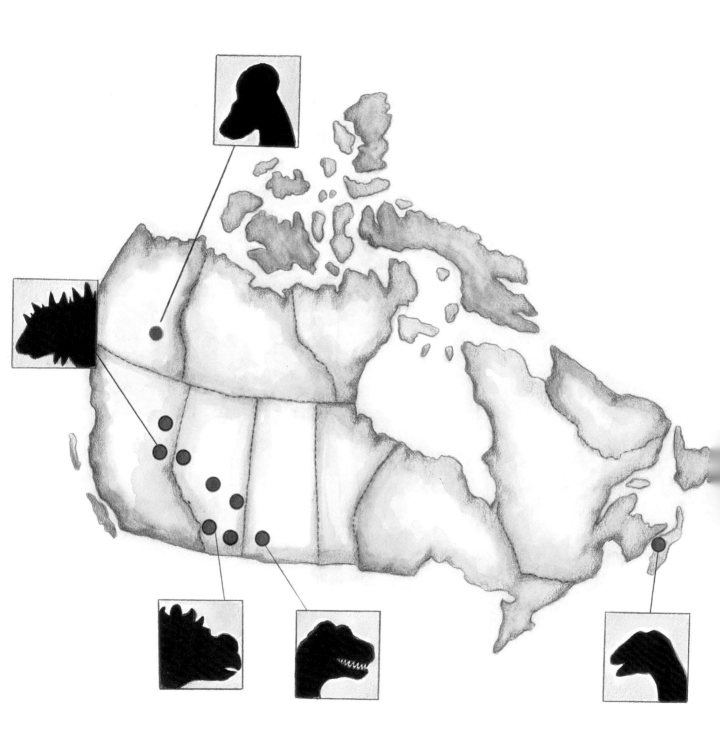

Dinosaurs across Canada

When it comes to dinosaur discoveries, Canada is one of the world's richest countries. More than 35 species, or kinds, have come from Dinosaur Provincial Park, Alberta, alone. Paleontologists recently discovered dinosaur tracks and duck-billed dinosaur bones in the Yukon and Northwest Territories. Saskatchewan rocks yielded a *Tyrannosaurus* (tye-RAN-oh-SORE-us). On the west coast of Nova Scotia lie rocks holding the oldest dinosaurs in Canada. Dinosaur footprints stroll across stones in the southern Canadian Rocky Mountains. In 1992, a single tooth belonging to a theropod (THER-oh-pod), or carnivorous dinosaur that walked on two legs, was found south of Courtenay on Vancouver Island, British Columbia.

Let's travel across the country and take a closer look at some of the coolest dinosaur finds in Canada!

> You will not find any dinosaur bones in the rocks beneath Toronto, Ottawa, or Montreal. Those cities were built on rocks formed during the last part of the Paleozoic era— before dinosaurs appeared.

Nova Scotia

Whew, it was hot! During the Late Triassic, from about 220 to 203 million years ago, the Fundy area of Nova Scotia was something like Death Valley, California today. Dry winds mounded reddish sand into dunes. Sometimes heavy rains created shallow lakes that slowly dried up, leaving behind sticky mudflats and white, mineral-crusted

> Some provinces, such as Ontario and Manitoba, don't have any dinosaur fossils. In fact, very few fossils from dinosaur times are found in eastern or central North America. Rocks that might have held them have eroded away.

soil. Bones and thousands of footprints uncovered by paleontologists show that dinosaurs walked through this harsh world.

The dinosaurs found in the Late Triassic rocks from Nova Scotia's west coast may be the oldest in North America. They include some of the first plant-eating dinosaurs, the prosauropods (proh-SORE-oh-podz). After biting off leaves and twigs, prosauropods relied on swallowed stones in their stomach to grind up the tough, stringy food.

Prosauropods, the first dinosaurs to weigh as much as an elephant, probably lived all over the world. They were replaced by giant sauropods (SORE-oh-podz), the group that includes *Diplodocus* (dih-PLOD-uh-kus) and *Apatosaurus* (ah-PAT-oh-SORE-us), in the Jurassic. Sometimes people think that all dinosaurs lived at the same time. But many different species of dinosaurs came and went during dinosaur times. The Fundy prosauropods lived about twice as many years before the more well-known *Tyrannosaurus* as *Tyrannosaurus* lived before us.

Unlike the scientists who discovered a T. rex in Saskatchewan, these paleontologists are in luck. The skull they are working on is in very good shape. Dinosaur fossils are often found in scattered pieces with parts missing, or in jumbles of crushed bones.

Saskatchewan

"Hey, I think I found something!" In 1991, two scientists from the Royal Saskatchewan Museum were looking for fossils in the Frenchman River valley near Eastend, Saskatchewan. A local schoolteacher, Robert Gebhart, had come with them to learn what fossils look like in the field. He spied some bone fragments and called the others to take a look. What Gebhart found turned out to be part of a *Tyrannosaurus rex*.

Excavation of the *T. rex*, now called "Scotty," did not begin until 1994. It took two years to complete. Not all of Scotty's skeleton was there and the bones that were present were jumbled together. The matrix (MAY-trix), or rock that held the bones, was very hard. Big pieces of matrix holding Scotty's bones were carefully removed, wrapped, and taken back to a laboratory. People have been working ever since to remove the bones from the rock.

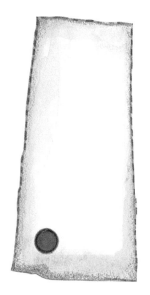

After Scotty was found, the Royal Saskatchewan Museum built a field station in Eastend so paleontologists could work where the fossils are. Field station scientists have uncovered the skeleton of a young duck-billed dinosaur showing an impression of its skin, *Triceratops* (try-SAIR-ah-tops) skulls, and the first ever *T. rex* coprolite. It is very unusual to be able to identify which species of dinosaur left behind a coprolite. How do paleontologists know this particular dropping belonged to a *T. rex*?

Paleontologist Karen Chin examined the 65-million-year-old, whitish-green fossil—about 2.4 litres (half a gallon) of petrified poop. She found it contained pieces of what appear to be *Triceratops* bone. The bone fragments mean the coprolite came from a carnivore, and *T. rex* is the only carnivore around at that time that was able to produce such super-sized poop.

By the way, *Tyrannosaurus rex* isn't the only dinosaur with two names—all living things have been given names with two parts. The first part, such as *Tyrannosaurus,* is called the genus (JEE-nus). A genus is a large group of very similar animals. Wolves, coyotes, and your pet poodle all belong to the genus *Canis* (KAY-nis). The second part of the name, the species, identifies the member of the genus. So you might hear a *Canis lupus* (wolf) howl or pet your *Canis familiaris* (dog). *Tyrannosaurus rex* means "tyrant lizard king."

Hidden away in the rocks of southwestern Saskatchewan is a wealth of information about the past 75 million years. Scientists have uncovered the fossils of land and sea dwellers from the end of the Cretaceous era, as well as those of strange-looking land animals that appeared after the dinosaurs were gone.

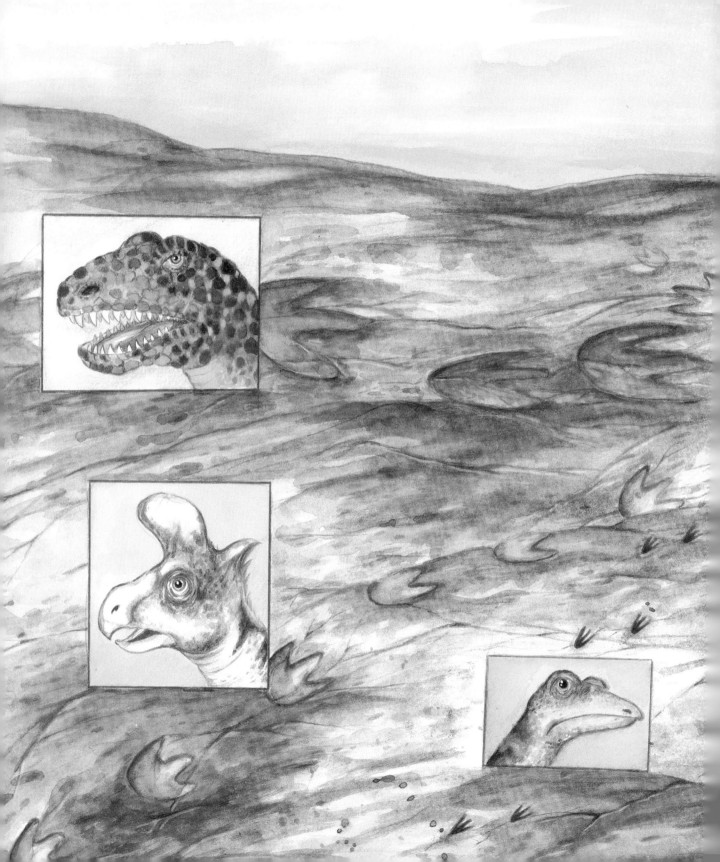

British Columbia

Eleven-year-old Mark Turner and nine-year-old Daniel Helm always enjoyed exploring the rocks around Tumbler Ridge, B.C. searching for dinosaur prints. In the summer of 2000, the pair found four slight hollows on a rock. On the advice of Rich McCrea, an expert on groups of dinosaur tracks called "trackways," the boys looked for more fossilized prints. They carefully measured and photographed what they found. From this information, McCrea figured out that the dinosaur that left the tracks was about 2 metres (6.6 feet) high at the hip and was moving along at about 2 kilometres (1.2 miles) per hour. McCrea and the boys uncovered a total of 26 footprints in the 95-million-year-old rocks—the first well-preserved trackway found in that set of rocks. McCrea also found some bits of dinosaur bone along the same surface, not far from the trackway. Bones and prints are rarely found together, making the site that Mark and Daniel discovered very important.

> People who study fossil tracks and other trace fossils, such as feeding marks or nests, are called ichnologists (ik-NAHL-oh-jists).

About 125 million years ago, the Peace River canyon area was warm, wet, and filled with plants. Lots of squishy mud made it a great place for dinosaurs to leave tracks. The tracks dried out and became hard. Then they were gently covered with more dirt and mud. The whole

Fossilized dinosaur footprints can tell scientists the size of the dinosaur that made them and how fast it was moving.

package was buried and turned to rock. Later, wind and water wore away the rock to uncover the ancient tracks.

In 1922, paleontologists identified fossil footprints from seven different kinds of dinosaurs in the rocks of the Peace River canyon. The site soon became world-famous for the many tracks that could be seen throughout the area. In the mid-1970s, paleontologist Philip Currie heard that a dam was to be built on the Peace River and would flood much of the canyon by 1979. He planned a rescue mission. Teams made several trips to the area, collecting about 80 footprints and making rubber molds of many more. They documented about 1700 footprints, including many trackways and some of the world's oldest bird footprints.

Eventually the dam was finished and the river began to fill up the canyon. Most of the remarkable dinosaur footprints disappeared under water. They can no longer be seen or studied, which is unfortunate because dinosaur trackways give us a great deal of information.

Measuring the distance between footprints can help us to figure out how fast dinosaurs walked and ran. The prints can also tell about how dinosaurs moved. The trackways of big sauropods don't include any tail drag marks, showing that they carried their long tails in the air. Some trackways tell a story: one from the Peace River canyon shows a group of herbivores moving along together and then all suddenly changing direction when a meat-eating dinosaur appears.

Leaving behind footprints in the squishy mud, Parasaurolophus moves through a warm, wet world. Millions of years later, those footprints reappear, preserved when the mud turned to rock.

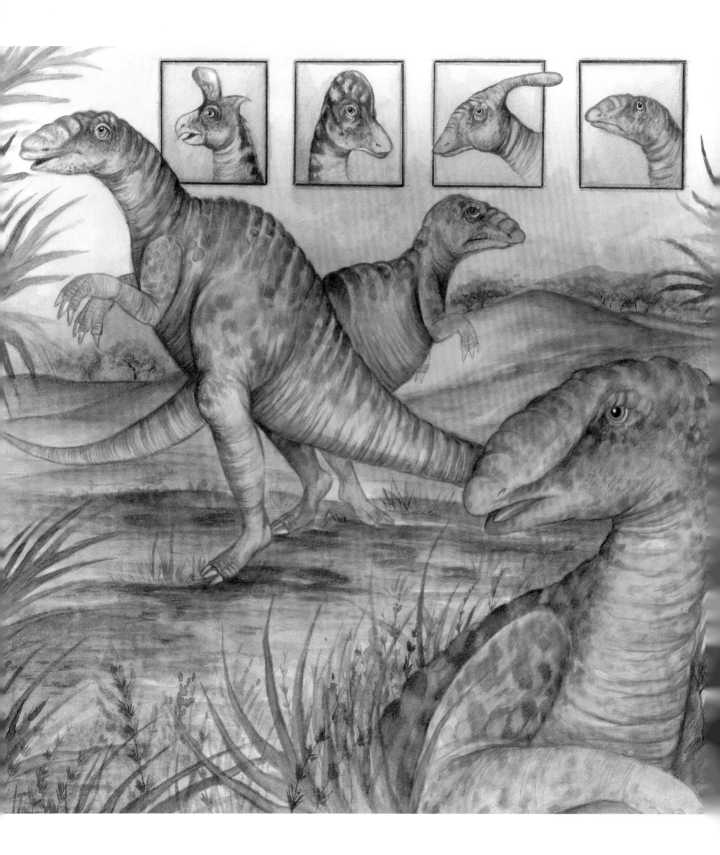

Alberta's Treasure Chest

The bizarre badlands along Alberta's Red Deer River are a dusty, dry place today. But if you had been there about 65 to 75 million years ago, you would have seen something more like the Gulf Coast of the United States. Big rivers wound through a landscape with many large swampy areas and fresh-water ponds. To the east was a great shallow inland sea. Plants grew well in the warm, wet climate. Flowering plants appeared for the first time during the Cretaceous period. They must have made a big change in how the world looked and smelled.

Plant-eating dinosaurs munched their way through the lush greenery. The herds of herbivores attracted the attention of carnivores, which sneakily stalked their prey. Dinosaurs and other animals died and were buried in layers of mud and sand. More and more layers piled up, burying the dinosaurs deeper. The mud and sand turned to rock, and the dinosaurs' bones became fossils. They stayed hidden in the earth until about a million years ago.

Like giant earthmovers, huge sheets of ice known as glaciers scraped away the overlying layers to reveal the Cretaceous rocks. When the glaciers melted about 15,000 to 10,000 years ago, they turned into lots and lots of water. The resulting floods ate away at the rocks, carving

Alberta was home to some dandy duck-billed dinosaurs. The small pictures show, from left to right, Lambeosaurus, Corythosaurus, Parasaurolophus, *and* Edmontosaurus, *who also walks through the large picture.*

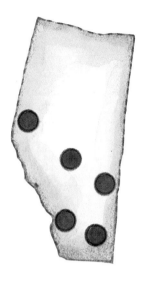

out a big channel that is now the Red Deer River valley. Since then, wind and water have kept nibbling away at the valley, creating the strange shapes of the badlands and bringing new fossils to the surface.

This is one of the best places in the world to find fossils. Horned dinosaurs, armoured dinosaurs, and duck-billed dinosaurs are all found here. Some are uncovered as single skeletons with their bones still close together. In other places, bones from many animals are concentrated in an area called a bone bed. Paleontologists know of more than 50 bone beds in Alberta's badlands. The bones may come from several kinds of dinosaurs and be so jumbled that it can be hard to sort them into individual animals.

Even more confusing are the bone beds that contain mainly one species. After finding a very rich *Centrosaurus* (sen-troh-SORE-us) bone bed, paleontologists came up with a clever way to count how many individual dinosaurs were there. As they excavated the bed, they watched for the piece of bone that forms the upper edge of the left eye socket. Each animal had only one of those. Every one they dug up would stand for a separate dinosaur—pretty smart! After 11 years, they had found 40 centrosaurs. From that, they estimated that the whole bone bed might hold 400.

Geologist Joseph Burr Tyrrell (TIR-ul) stumbled across the first dinosaur here in 1884. It was a 70-million-year-old carnivore skull belonging to what would later be named *Albertosaurus* (al-BUR-toh-SORE-rus). In 1898, Lawrence Lambe (LAM) came to the Red Deer River valley looking for dinosaur fossils and found several single bones. Not much else happened in the badlands until 1909. A fossil hunter working for the American Museum of Natural History, Barnum Brown, made a quick trip to the area to check out a rancher's story about huge bones. What Brown saw kicked off "The Great Canadian Dinosaur Rush."

The next summer, Brown came back with three assistants. He had carpenters build a big raft that would hold supplies, a tent, and whatever bones they might find. Brown's party floated down the Red Deer River collecting fossils as they went. When he spotted bone fragments at the base of a slope, Brown scrambled up to find the rocks they had come from. After gently clearing off the bone-holding rock, Brown would decide whether to dig. Picks and shovels, even dynamite, were used to clear away overlying dirt and rock. Brown's crew was more careful closer to the bones. They used hammers and chisels to free pieces of rock holding the bones. The big chunks of rock and bone were wrapped in burlap soaked in plaster. Then the men packed them in hay-filled boxes. A skeleton could be uncovered in three days, but it might take three weeks of hard work to get it ready to be shipped.

Brown returned each summer through 1915. He shipped boxcars of

A ship carrying a load of dinosaur bones collected by Charles Sternberg for the British Museum of Natural History was sunk by a German submarine in 1916. Sternberg said the lost fossils were some of the best he had ever found.

bones back to New York. Altogether, Brown gathered 300 large cases of fossils, including the complete skeletons of 14 big dinosaurs. Canadians worried that all of their fossils were being shipped out of the country. The government hired its own team, the Sternberg family from Kansas, to go out to Alberta and dig up some dinosaurs for Canadian museums.

In the summer of 1912, Charles Sternberg and his two sons, Levi and Charlie, travelled to the Red Deer River valley to collect for the Geological Survey of Canada. In August, they found a complete skeleton of a new type of duck-billed dinosaur not far from Drumheller. It was later named *Edmontosaurus* (ed-MON-toh-SORE-us).

During the next few summers, the Sternbergs continued their prospecting. They often worked close to Barnum Brown's camp. Luckily, there were so many bones that everyone managed to get along. The great bone rush ended in 1915, but paleontologists continued to find many dinosaurs in the badlands.

Dinosaur Provincial Park

What do Alberta's badlands and Egypt's pyramids have in common? They are both recognized as treasures belonging to the whole world. In 1979, the United Nations named Dinosaur Provincial Park a World Heritage Site, just like the Egyptian pyramids, making it the first place listed for its fossils.

The park covers more than 7000 hectares (16,000 acres) along the Red Deer River in central southern Alberta. Paleontologists working from the Royal Tyrrell Museum's field station in the park are always searching for fossils. They set up digs on the sites that look the most promising. People who want to try being paleontologists can take part in one of the field programs run by the Royal Tyrrell Museum.

The rocks of the badlands have yielded nearly 300 species of fossil plants and animals. According to the bones, some pretty cool dinosaurs lived here about 75 million years ago during the Cretaceous period: duck-bills, horned heads, boneheads, armour wearers, bird-mimics, and meat-munchers. In the next section, you'll get to know them better!

Duck-billed Dinosaurs

Hadrosaurs (HAD-roh-sorz) were plant-eating dinosaurs. Their long, broad snouts ended in a wide, toothless beak that looked a bit like a duck's bill. Because of that, hadrosaurs are nicknamed "duck-bills." The duck-bills' tough beaks were good for nipping off bits of plants. Inside their mouths were some truly awesome sets of teeth. Each working tooth had three to five more replacements stacked underneath it. A person has 32 teeth. A duck-bill's mouth might have 2000 teeth crammed inside!

There were two types of duck-bills, and both lived in Alberta—the world's richest location of hadrosaur fossils. Some, such as *Hadrosaurus* (HAD-roh-SORE-us), had flattened heads. *Lambeosaurus* (LAM-bee-oh-SORE-us) and others had weird, hollow head crests of many different shapes. Paleontologists think that dinosaurs may have used them to make noises something like an elephant trumpeting.

Growing up to 13 metres (42 feet) long—about the size of a school bus—with a head the size of a horse's, *Edmontosaurus* was one of Alberta's biggest hadrosaurs. It had bumpy, leathery skin and, although it lacked a head crest, a fleshy frill ran down its back and tail. Crisscrossing tendons filled the tail, making it very stiff and hard to bend. *Edmontosaurus* moved along slowly,

A Corythosaurus *parent brings tender leaves and twigs to the nest for the young duckbills. Some dinosaur species nested in colonies, just as birds such as pelicans and gulls do today.*

eating plants. It probably relied on good eyesight, hearing, and smell to keep away from predators. Canadian paleontologist Lawrence Lambe named this dinosaur for the Edmonton Formation rocks in which its bones were found.

In 1898, Lambe unearthed the first duck-billed dinosaur bones found in North America and the species, *Lambeosaurus,* was named in his honour. It had a large, thin, wedge-shaped crest that tilted forward. A long spike jutted out the back. *Lambeosaurus* is one of the biggest known duck-bills. Some measured about 15 metres (50 feet) long from head to tail. Like other hadrosaurs, lambeosaurs appear to have travelled together in herds. Large hadrosaur herds may have migrated long distances. They could have followed changing food supplies as caribou herds do today.

Barnum Brown thought the crest of a hadrosaur he found in Alberta looked like an ancient Greek soldier's helmet. He named it *Corythosaurus* (koh-RITH-oh-SORE-us)—"helmeted lizard." Like other duck-bills, *Corythosaurus* probably walked on two legs, but may have dropped to all fours when grazing. It weighed about as much as an elephant.

Still more duck-bills roamed the area. *Parasaurolophus* (PAR-ah-sore-OL-oh-fus) was about as long as two cars. It had a hollow bony crest up to 1.8 metres (6 feet) long—longer than the rest of its head. The oldest hadrosaur found in Alberta so far is *Prosaurolophus* (PROH-sore-OL-oh-fus). It lived there about 75 million years ago and was slightly smaller than *Parasaurolophus*.

In 1911, Barnum Brown collected the first nearly complete dinosaur skeleton found in Canada. It belonged to a duck-bill later named *Saurolophus* (sore-OL-oh-fus). The find even showed rare skin impressions. Traces of the skin could also be seen on the *Gryposaurus* (GRYE-poh-SORE-us) found by George Sternberg in 1913. This dinosaur had small, smooth scales on its neck, sides, and stomach.

Charles Sternberg discovered yet another Alberta hadrosaur species in 1936. *Brachylophosaurus* (BRACK-ih-LOH-fuh-SORE-us) was about 7 metres (22 feet) long and only weighed about half as much as some of the largest duck-bills.

Horned Dinosaurs

Ceratopians (SER-uh-TOP-ee-inz) means "horned faces." Take a look and you can see how these rhinoceros-like dinosaurs got their name. They were plant-eaters with beaks like parrots and teeth that worked like scissors. Horned dinosaurs lived in a variety of habitats. And there were a lot of horned dinosaurs: near the end of the

In 1987, a teenager helped to discover Canada's first dinosaur nest site. It was in Alberta's badlands, but not in Dinosaur Provincial Park. While exploring near the Milk River in southern Alberta, in an area called Devil's Coulee (KOO-lee), Wendy Sloboda found what she thought might be pieces of dinosaur eggshell. When paleontologists visited the site, they found nests, eggs, and lots of baby duck-billed dinosaur bones. Some of the eggs still held the tiny bones of unborn baby hadrosaurs! The nests may have been made by *Hypacrosaurus* (hye-PAK-roh-SORE-us), a duckbill 9 metres (30 feet) long, with a narrow, bony crest. The province quickly bought the site to protect and preserve the remarkable find.

Cretaceous period, they made up half or more of the total known dinosaur population! They were some of the last non-bird dinosaurs to appear.

Triceratops weighed more than an elephant and was nearly as long as a city bus. Its skull was about 2 metres (6 feet) long. Slightly smaller, *Chasmosaurus* (KAZ-moh-SORE-us) had a 1.5-metre-long (5-foot-long) head: over half of that length was made up by its neck frill. Like the other ceratopians, *Triceratops* and *Chasmosaurus* had short, sturdy legs and stout four-toed feet.

Styracosaurus (sty-RACK-oh-SORE-us) had a large nose horn and six long spikes sticking out from the back edge of its neck frill. These horns and spikes could have been helpful in fighting off predators, but they may have had another use as well. Paleontologists think that some horned dinosaurs lived in herds. They might have acted much like herd animals today. Male styracosaurs wanting to be boss may have lowered their heads to display their spikes and walked toward one another. If one of them did not turn away, the two may have pushed and shoved each

> Ceratopians never ran out of sharp teeth. Their jaws held columns of teeth something like those of the duck-bills— at least three in each stack. When a tooth wore out from grinding up plants, it fell out and a new one replaced it.

A Pachyrhinosaurus *herd contained animals of all ages. Evidence that some dinosaurs lived and travelled in herds comes from trackways and from bone beds that contain the remains of many individuals of the same species.*

other until one quit. It could have proved quite a contest: an adult *Styracosaurus* could weigh up to 2700 kilograms (3 tons) and measure 5.5 metres (18 feet) long.

One of the reasons for believing some horned dinosaurs lived in herds is that their fossils are often found in bone beds containing the remains of many individuals of the same species. Samples from three *Centrosaurus* bone beds in Dinosaur Provincial Park show that each one might hold the remains of 300 to 1000 animals.

Some of the bones in one *Centrosaurus* bed were broken soon after the animals died. Paleontologists who have studied the site think a *Centrosaurus* herd may have been trying to cross a river and drowned. Imagine a panicking herd of these 6-metre-long (20-foot-long) dinosaurs! Scared animals may have stepped on others as they scrambled to escape. The same kind of event is also believed to be responsible for some other bone beds.

Near Grande Prairie, Alberta, paleontologists found a bone bed containing a *Pachyrhinosaurus* (PAK-ih-RYE-noh-SORE-us) herd that lived about 85 million years ago. The 2200 bones excavated here belonged to pachyrhinosaurs of all different sizes. This horned dinosaur was about the same size as *Centrosaurus*, but had a rough, thick knob of bone on its snout instead of a nose horn.

Boneheaded Dinosaurs

Pachycephalosaurus (PACK-ih-SEF-uh-loh-SORE-us) was a bonehead! The top of its skull was round and hard like a bowling ball, thanks to a bone roof 20 centimetres (8 inches) thick. There were bony ridges along the side of its head and over its eyes. Bumps and spikes of different sizes stuck out of its head. *Pachycephalosaurus* was about 5 metres (15 feet) long. It was the biggest of the bone-heads, or pachycephalosaurs. *Stegoceras* (steg-OSS-er-us) was only about half as long. But it still had 6 centimetres (2½ inches) of bone on the top of its head. Another Alberta pachycephalosaur, *Ornatotholus* (or-NATE-oh-THOH-lus), was only about 1.5 metres (5 feet) long.

The boneheads had horny beaks and small, sharp, leaf-shaped cheek teeth. They probably ate mostly plants and maybe a few insects or small animals. Pachycephalosaurs walked on their strong hind legs. Their straight, stiff tails helped them to keep their balance. Their arms were small and ended in five-fingered hands. Boneheads probably ran away if they saw or smelled danger. They did not have any real defenses.

Why did these dinosaurs have such thick skulls? Paleontologists used to think bonehead males may have butted heads like male bighorn sheep do today. But bighorn sheep skulls

We know little about the boneheads because pachy-cephalosaur skeletons are very rare. Only two good ones have been found: one from Alberta and one from Mongolia. Paleontologists usually find only the bony skullcap of these thick-headed dinosaurs.

have a wide area for making contact, while the top of a pachycephalosaur's skull is round like a bowling ball. This would only give a small area of contact and put a great deal of strain on the dinosaur's neck. So now some scientists believe the boneheads are more likely to have butted each other's bodies. No one knows for sure.

Armoured Dinosaurs

Imagine a walking tank 7 metres (23 feet) long and weighing 4000 kilograms (4½ tons). *Edmontonia* (ED-mon-TOH-nee-uh) was a heavily armoured, barrel-bodied, plant-eating dinosaur. Spikes and bony plates, called scutes (SKOOTS), protected its back and sides. Large bony scales on its head protected its brain from a predator's bite. It even had rows of small, pointed plates running down its tail.

Edmontonia had short legs that kept it close to the ground. It could probably only reach the bottom 2 metres (7 feet) of plants. With its narrow, toothless beak, *Edmontonia* would have nipped off bites of soft, juicy plants such as ferns or the flowering plants that had only recently appeared. Its small cheek teeth would have sliced up the food a bit, but the main work of turning the food to pulp was done by its gut.

A slow-moving dinosaur, *Edmontonia* relied on its armour for protection from predators. The long, sharp

Exactly what Pachycephalosaurus *did with its thick-boned skull is a mystery that may never be solved.*

spikes on its shoulders would have been very dangerous to an attacking predator.

Another Alberta armoured plant-eater lacked shoulder spikes, but had a strong tail ending in a bony club that could weigh up to 30 kilograms (65 pounds). *Euoplocephalus* (YOO-oh-ploh-SEF-uh-lus) probably swung its club from side to side, whacking any predator that came too close. It could hit hard enough to break the leg of an attacking tyrannosaur. When *Euoplocephalus* was threatened, it would likely have turned to keep its tail club toward the attacker, relying on its flexible bony armour to protect it from bites. About the same size as *Edmontonia, Euoplocephalus* had a larger, heavier beak but probably ate the same foods.

Bird-mimic Dinosaurs

The ornithomimids (OR-nith-oh-MYE-midz) or "bird-mimic" dinosaurs were built a lot like ostriches. A fossil discovered in Alberta in 1995 showed that they even had toothless beaks covered in keratin (KAIR-uh-tin). Keratin is the horny substance that makes up hair, fingernails, and bird beaks. Unlike ostriches, these dinosaurs had long tails that could be held out behind them when they ran,

Slow-moving Edmontonia *could not run away from danger, but its armour of bony plates and wicked shoulder spikes offered good protection from predators.*

helping to balance their head and long neck. Instead of wings, they had long, thin arms ending in three spindly fingers tipped with slightly curved claws.

Struthiomimus (strooth-ee-oh-MYE-mus), the "ostrich mimic," stood about 2 metres (7 feet) tall and measured about 3.7 metres (12 feet) from nose to tail tip. Like other ornithomimids, it had hollow bones and a thin skull, making it light for its size. Combine low weight with long hind legs designed for sprinting and you get a very fast animal!

Ornithomimids were probably the fastest of all dinosaurs. Some scientists think *Dromiceiomimus* (droh-MEE-see-uh-MYE-mus) may have been able to run as fast as an ostrich—up to 80 kilometres (50 miles) per hour over short distances. Their speed would have come in handy for escaping predators.

Paleontologists have long believed that ornithomimids probably ate plants, small animals, and insects. But recent fossil finds suggest a different diet. Two ornithomimid skulls, one of them an *Ornithomimus* (or-nith-oh-MYE-mus) from Alberta, show traces of a comblike filter on the beak. *Ornithomimus,* which stood about 2.7 metres

Built for speed with long legs and light bones, the ornithomimids, or "bird mimics," were probably the fastest of all dinosaurs.

(9 feet) tall, and its relatives may have fed in much the same way as ducks and flamingoes. These birds suck water that contains food into their mouths, then force the water out through fine hairs surrounding their beaks, leaving the food behind. Another piece of evidence that suggests this new idea may be correct is the fact that ornithomimid fossils are commonly found in rocks formed in wet environments but are very rarely seen in those from dry habitats.

Meat-munching Dinosaurs

Some fierce carnivores were hunting in Alberta 65 to 75 million years ago. One of them may be the most famous dinosaur in the world, even though it was only around for the last three million years of dinosaur time.

Tyrannosaurus rex was one of the biggest meat-eaters ever to walk on Earth. Weighing as much as an elephant, it measured 12 to 15 metres (40 to 50 feet) long. It walked on powerful hind legs, leaning forward with its tail up and out to help balance its heavy head, which was an impressive 1.5 metres (5 feet) long. Its very small but strong arms ended in two clawed fingers.

Tyrannosaurus had 50 to 60 teeth as big as bananas inside a mouth the size of a bathtub. Each tooth was shaped like a steak knife and had the same kind of serrated edge to slice through flesh and bone. Scientists using real bones and models of tyrannosaur teeth have shown that *T. rex* could bite harder than any animal alive today. It was strong enough to chomp through *Triceratops* bones. And *Tyrannosaurus* took big bites: a single mouthful of meat and bone could weigh more than 100 kilograms (220 pounds). That's like gulping down 880 burgers at once!

Did *Tyrannosaurus* hunt and kill animals or just look for dead animals to eat? Like many of today's carnivores, it probably did both. It had big eyes and a good sense of smell for finding prey. But could *Tyrannosaurus* catch a fleeing dinosaur? Scientists have different ideas about how fast *Tyrannosaurus* could move. Some say it could only manage a fast walk, while others think it could run quickly in short bursts when chasing prey.

In 1981, paleontologists discovered what turned out to be most of a *T. rex* skeleton in the Crowsnest Pass area of Alberta. The tyrannosaur was nicknamed "Black Beauty" because of the dark colour of its mineral-stained bones.

Eight million years before *Tyrannosaurus* appeared, its relative *Albertosaurus* was already hunting herbivores. Standing about 2.5 metres (8 feet) high at the hip, *Albertosaurus* was smaller than *Tyrannosaurus* but every bit as ferocious a hunter.

In 1910, Barnum Brown found a bunch of *Albertosaurus* fossils jumbled together at a site in Alberta's badlands. He sent bones to the American Museum of Natural History and then more or less forgot about the whole thing. When Canadian paleontologist Philip

Albertosaurus ("Alberta lizard") was named the same year that Alberta became a province—1905.

Currie tried to find the site in 1997, he ran into a problem: Brown had not written down the location. But he had taken photographs. Currie and his team searched the badlands to find landmarks that matched those in the pictures. Eventually they succeeded. So far, parts of at least a dozen *Albertosaurus* skeletons have been unearthed. This find is important because it is one of the only sites in the world showing that tyrannosaurs like *Albertosaurus* may have lived and hunted in packs.

Another tyrannosaur, *Daspletosaurus* (das-PLEE-toh-SORE-us) lived about the same time as *Albertosaurus* and looked rather like it. The two predators are probably closely related.

A smaller Alberta carnivore, *Troodon* (TROH-oh-don), was probably one of the smartest of all the dinosaurs. *Troodon* was about the size of a person and had a brain as big as an emu's—very large for its body size compared to other dinosaurs. It was probably at least as smart as an ostrich. Some scientists think *Troodon* may have been clever enough to hunt in packs.

Troodon had large eyes—each nearly 5 centimetres (2 inches) wide — that would have been good for spotting prey. Such big eyes may mean that it did its hunting in low light, perhaps at dawn and dusk. With its long legs

Carnivorous dinosaurs came in all sizes. Here a little Troodon, *about the same size as a person, darts past a* Tyrannosaurus *that's 12 metres (40 feet) long.*

An Asian relative of *Dromaeosaurus, Velociraptor* (vuh-LAH-sih-RAP-tor), became famous in the movie *Jurassic Park. Velociraptor* fossils have been found in Mongolia, Russia, and China.

and tail to help it balance, *Troodon* could move quickly and make sharp turns. Its three long, clawed fingers allowed it to snatch up small reptiles, mammals, and birds. *Troodon* had sharp, curved, serrated teeth: its name means "wounding tooth."

Like hadrosaurs, *Troodon* nested in colonies. Paleontologists who have studied both nesting areas believe that tough little *Troodon* babies were much more capable of caring for themselves than baby duck-bills were.

Dromaeosaurus (DROH-mee-oh-SORE-us) may have been small—about the size of a person—but it was fast and deadly. Each hind foot had an extra-long, switchblade-like claw on the second toe. This was probably used for ripping the guts out of prey. If that's not scary enough, *Dromaeosaurus* also had hooked claws on its three fingers and a mouthful of big fangs.

Extinction

Species die out, or go extinct, when they cannot adapt to changes in their environment or when they lose the competition for resources to other organisms. The fossil record shows that extinction is a natural process: more than 99 percent of all species that have ever lived have become extinct. Most extinctions happen gradually over time, but sometimes many species go extinct at once. The biggest mass extinction of all time happened 250 million years ago. As many as 95 percent of the species on Earth may have died.

How and why this happened is something scientists are still trying to figure out. No one idea seems to tell the whole story. The same thing is true for the final cause of the non-bird dinosaurs' disappearance 65 million years ago. Most dinosaur species had disappeared through gradual extinction well before the end of the Cretaceous period. Scientists have several ideas about what might have happened to the rest of them.

One theory is that an asteroid from outer space crashed into Earth. Along with other evidence, scientists discovered a crater 200 kilometres (120 miles) wide and about 65 million years old in the Gulf of Mexico. An impact that large would have immediately and drastically changed the environment, throwing huge clouds of debris into the atmosphere, starting fires, and causing earthquakes and giant waves. Dust clouds would

> **Other forms of life died out about the same time as the dinosaurs: flying reptiles, some mammal and plant species, as well as many kinds of sea life.**

have darkened skies for months, blocking sunlight and lowering temperatures. Plants, unable to make food, would have died. Plant-eating animals would soon have starved. Meat-eaters left without their normal prey would have turned on one another, eventually all dying out.

Some scientists think this alone caused the dinosaurs to become extinct. Others think that the dinosaurs were already having trouble adapting to changing conditions and that the asteroid just finished them off.

Volcanoes were very active during the late Cretaceous period, throwing a great deal of dust and acid chemicals into the air. This could have caused the same kind of effects as debris from an asteroid, as well as creating acid rain. The great seas were shrinking, possibly allowing migrating dinosaurs to mix with each other for the first time. Diseases or new predators may have killed off many dinosaurs. No one knows how many dinosaurs were around at the very end, but *Tyrannosaurus* and *Triceratops* were among the last of their kind.

Are the dinosaurs losers because they became extinct? No. They ruled the land for most of the 160 million years they were around. And technically, they are still around, perched in the trees as birds.

Figuring out the Past

When you read about dinosaurs, you might wonder how we know so much about creatures that died so long ago. The answers are in the rocks and bones.

Paleontologists pay attention to many details at a fossil site. They examine the rocks the bones are in for such things as raindrop impressions, mud cracks, or plant fossils that can tell them what the environment was like when the rocks formed. They look for clues that tell them how the bones came to be in that place. This information can give paleontologists clues about an animal's lifestyle.

Dinosaur teeth tell us what kind of food they ate. Large, pointed teeth meant for stabbing and tearing belonged to a carnivore. Herbivores had flatter teeth designed for shredding and grinding up plants. Sometimes paleontologists can actually see what dinosaurs ate. One small dinosaur was found with lizard bones in its belly. A tooth from a tyrannosaur was found stuck in a duck-bill's leg bone. Tooth marks on other kinds of bones have also been matched to tyrannosaurs. And remember the *T. rex* coprolite containing *Triceratops* bone (see Saskatchewan section).

New technologies help paleontologists get more information from fossils. Some fossils, such as dinosaur skulls or eggs, may be too rare or delicate to risk opening to find out what's inside. Paleontologists can use a CAT scan, which doctors use to see inside human bodies, to look

inside the fossil without harming it. A CAT scan (computerized axial tomography) is an X-ray technique that creates three dimensional images. A scan of a dinosaur egg might show the bones of the baby dinosaur curled up inside.

Some computer programs take an object and "morph" it into another, showing step by step how the change happened. Paleontologists use these programs to get an idea of what a dinosaur looked like as it grew from baby to adult.

How do artists go from bare bones to real-looking pictures and models? Artists work with paleontologists to come up with accurate pictures of dinosaurs. By looking at scars on the bones, paleontologists can see how muscles were attached. An artist who wants to show what a dinosaur looked like when it was alive will first figure out the shape of its muscles as they lie over the bones.

Imagining what dinosaur skin looked like is a bit trickier. For a few species, we have skin impressions. For the rest, the artist must guess based on what scientists know about dinosaurs and living reptiles. Skin colour is an even bigger guess. But scientists recently found a way to figure out what colour a 350-million-year-old fish was. Maybe dinosaurs will be next.

Everything we know about dinosaurs and their world has been learned by paleontologists carefully studying fossils. Even a single dinosaur tooth can reveal whether the owner ate plants or meat. Herbivore teeth are flat for grinding and mashing. Carnivore teeth are sharp and pointed, for ripping and tearing.

From Discovery to Display

So you want to find a dinosaur, dig it up, bring it home, and set up the skeleton in your room. How do you begin? And what kind of jobs will you have to do?

Paleontologists searching for dinosaurs start by finding rocks that are the right age and type to have dinosaur fossils in them. Then they do a lot of walking around, watching for bits of bone poking out of the rocks or lying on the ground. You might even see a paleontologist licking a piece of rock. What is she doing? Fossil bone and rock look a lot alike but rock doesn't stick to your tongue—bone does!

Before anything is moved from where it lies, paleontologists make a record of the site. They often grid it off into measured squares. Then they take photographs, make careful drawings, or use electronic measuring tools to enter location information right into a computer. The paleontologists note where each new bone is found.

Everything from bulldozers and jackhammers to small chisels and soft brushes may be used to get rid of excess rock and dirt. When the fossil is free, it is wrapped in a jacket of plaster—very much like the cast put on a broken human bone. Now the fossil can be shipped to a lab.

The delicate work of separating bone from rock takes place at the lab. A preparator (pruh-PAIR-uh-tor) carefully unwraps the fossil. Then he slowly removes rock from around the bone, often using tools like those your dentist uses. Sometimes the preparator views the fossil under a microscope and works with a very fine needle. This job takes lots of patience! The cleaned fossil is protected with a coat of clear glue. Only when the fossil is clean will the paleontologists know exactly what they have found.

Paleontologists rarely find complete skeletons. For display specimens, missing bones are often replaced with models or bones from another dinosaur of the same kind. Fibreglass models of bones are often used instead of the real bones. Fibreglass weighs much less and is easier to handle. The bones are attached, one by one, to a steel framework.

Royal Tyrrell Museum of Paleontology

Located in Alberta's badlands near Drumheller, the Royal Tyrrell Museum is one of the best places in the world to learn about dinosaurs and other ancient life. Scientists at the museum collect, study, write about, and display fossils from Alberta and elsewhere.

The museum opened in 1985. Its name honours Joseph Tyrrell, who found the first dinosaur skeleton from this area in 1884, not far from where the museum now sits.

More than 200 dinosaur specimens are on display. Most have come from the surrounding badlands. A special exhibit on theropods highlights *Tyrannosaurus rex* and other carnivores. Other exhibits illustrate life on Earth before and after the time of the dinosaurs.

Dinosaur People Past and Present

Canada's Native peoples were the first to see huge bones weathering out from the rocks. The Piikani said they belonged to "the grandfather of the buffalo" and honoured the ancient spirit by leaving offerings.

In 1874, geologist George Mercer Dawson was working with the Boundary Commission in what are now Saskatchewan and Alberta. He found the first Canadian dinosaur fossils in the badlands of south central Saskatchewan.

Despite the fact that a world-famous dinosaur museum bears his name, Joseph Burr Tyrrell was not a paleontologist. The 1884 *Albertosaurus* skull was his only dinosaur find. Tyrrell was a respected explorer and mining engineer.

Famous fossil finder Barnum Brown was nicknamed "Mr. Bones." He discovered many dinosaurs, including the first *Tyrannosaurus rex*. Brown searched for fossils in hard-to-reach places around the world. He collected in the Alberta badlands from 1911 to 1915.

Working about the same time as Barnum Brown, Charles Hazelius Sternberg and his three paleontologist sons dug up fossils to sell to whomever would buy them. If Sternberg could not sell his finds, he got no money. He was often poor. The family's most famous discovery was a fossilized *Edmontosaurus* from Wyoming that showed detailed skin impressions.

Lawrence Lambe was Canada's first real dinosaur paleontologist. He explored the Alberta badlands during the late 1800s and early 1900s. He recognized how important these deposits were. Lambe described and named several dinosaur species, including *Chasmosaurus, Edmontosaurus, Euoplocephalus, Stegoceras,* and *Styracosaurus.*

Barnum Brown at the site of a dinosaur excavation in Drumheller, Alberta.
(Glenbow Museum, NA-937-10)

American fossil hunter "Charlie" Sternberg (son of Charles Hazelius Sternberg) came to Canada to find fossils in 1912 and stayed. He became a Canadian citizen and worked as a collector for the Canadian Geological Survey. Charlie named *Edmontonia* and *Pachyrhinosaurus,* as well as other dinosaurs.

When six-year-old Philip Currie found a plastic triceratops in a box of Rice Krispies, it was the start of a lifelong connection with dinosaurs. Currie is now a paleontologist at the Royal Tyrrell Museum and has done extensive digging in the Alberta badlands. He has recently been working in China on feathered dinosaurs.

Where Can I Learn More?

- Check out the great dinosaur books, videos, and CD-ROMs at your local library.
- Visit the places listed below in person or on-line.

In Canada:

Canadian Museum of Nature
P.O. Box 3443, Station D
Ottawa, ON K1P 6P4
http://nature.ca

Dinosaur Provincial Park—World Heritage Site
P.O. Box 60
Patricia, AB T0J 2K0
http://www.cd.gov.ab.ca/parks/dinosaur

Fundy Geological Museum
162 Two Island Road
P.O. Box 640
Parrsboro, NS B0M 1S0
http://museum.gov.ns.ca/fgm/index.html

Royal Ontario Museum
Main Building
100 Queen's Park
Toronto, ON M5S 2C6
http://www.rom.on.ca

Royal Saskatchewan Museum
2445 Albert Street
Regina, SK S4P 3V7
http://www.royalsaskmuseum.ca

Royal Tyrrell Museum
P.O. Box 7500
Drumheller, AB T0J 0Y0
http://www.tyrrellmuseum.com

T. rex Discovery Centre
P.O. Box 646
Eastend, SK S0N 0T0
http://www.dinocountry.com/
   t-rex_center.html

In the United States:

American Museum of Natural History
Central Park West at 79th Street
New York, NY 10024-5192
http://www.amnh.org

Dinosaur National Monument
4545 East Highway 40
Dinosaur, CO 81610-9724
http://www.nps.gov/dino/index.htm

Dinosaur National Monument (Quarry)
11625 East 1500 South
Jensen, UT 84035
http://www.nps.gov/dino/dinos.htm

Field Museum of Natural History
1400 South Lake Shore Drive
Chicago, IL 60605-2496
http://www.fmnh.org

Smithsonian Institution National Museum
   of Natural History
10th Street and Constitution Avenue, NW
Washington, DC 20560
http://www.mnh.si.edu

In CyberSpace:

Dino Data
http://www.dinodata.net

Zoom Dinosaurs
http://www.EnchantedLearning.com/
  subjects/dinosaurs

Glossary and Pronunciation Guide

Albertosaurus (al-BUR-toh-SORE-rus)

Brachylophosaurus (BRACK-ih-LOH-fuh-SORE-us)

carnivore (KAR-nih-vor): meat eater
Cenozoic (sen-uh-ZOH-ik) era: 65 million years ago
    to present
Centrosaurus (sen-troh-SORE-us)
ceratopian (SER-uh-TOP-ee-in): horned dinosaur
Chasmosaurus (KAZ-moh-SORE-us)
coprolite (KOH-proh-lite): fossilized droppings (feces)
Corythosaurus (koh-RITH-oh-SORE-us)
Cretaceous (kree-TAY-shus) period: 135–65 million years ago

Daspletosaurus (das-PLEE-toh-SORE-us)
Dromaeosaurus (DROH-mee-oh-SORE-us)
Dromiceiomimus (droh-MEE-see-uh-MYE-mus)

Edmontonia (ED-mon-TOH-nee-uh)
Edmontosaurus (ed-MON-toh-SORE-us)
Euoplocephalus (YOO-oh-ploh-SEF-uh-lus)

Gryposaurus (GRYE-poh-SORE-us)

hadrosaur (HAD-roh-sore): duck-billed dinosaur
Hadrosaurus (HAD-roh-SORE-us)
herbivore (HER-bih-vor): plant eater
Hypacrosaurus (hye-PAK-roh-SORE-us)

ichnologist (ik-NAHL-oh-jist): scientist who studies trace
    fossils such as dinosaur tracks and nests

Jurassic (jur-ASS-ik) period: 203–135 million years ago

keratin (KAIR-uh-tin): material that makes up bird beaks
    and fingernails

Lambeosaurus (LAM-bee-oh-SORE-us)

Mesozoic (mez-oh-ZOH-ik) era: *250–65* million years ago

Ornatotholus (or-NATE-oh-THOH-lus)
ornithischian (or-nih-THIS-kee-an): dinosaur with
    birdlike hips
ornithomimid (OR-nith-oh-MYE-mid): "bird-mimic"
    dinosaur
Ornithomimus (OR-nith-oh-MYE-mus)

pachycephalosaur (PACK-ih-SEF-uh-loh-SORE):
    bone-headed dinosaur
Pachycephalosaurus (PACK-ih-SEF-uh-loh-SORE-us)
Pachyrhinosaurus (PAK-ih-RYE-noh-SORE-us)

paleontologist (pale-ee-on-TAHL-uh-jist): scientist who
    studies ancient life
Paleozoic (pale-ee-uh-ZOH-ik) era: 540–250 million
    years ago
Parasaurolophus (PAR-ah-sore-OL-oh-fus)
preparator (pruh-PAIR-uh-tor): person who removes fossils
    from rock and prepares them for study and display
Prosaurolophus (PROH-sore-OL-oh-fus)
prosauropod (proh-SORE-oh-pod): an early plant-eating
    dinosaur

saurischian (sore-IS-kee-an): dinosaur with lizard-like hips
sauropod (SORE-oh-pod): giant plant-eating dinosaur
Saurolophus (sore-OL-oh-fus)
scutes (SKOOTS): bony plates
Stegoceras (steg-OSS-er-us)
Struthiomimus (strooth-ee-oh-MYE-mus)
Styracosaurus (sty-RACK-oh-SORE-us)

theropod (THER-oh-pod): carnivorous dinosaur that
    walked on two legs
Triassic (try-ASS-ik) period: 250–203 million years ago
Triceratops (try-SAIR-ah-tops)
Troodon (TROH-oh-don)
Tyrannosaurus (tye-RAN-oh-SORE-us)

Velociraptor (vuh-LAH-sih-RAP-tor)

Index

Numbers in **bold** refer to illustrations

About the Author

Rebecca Grambo has written more than 20 books for children and adults. Her titles include *Borealis: A Polar Bear Cub's First Year* and *Weird Science*. She studied geological engineering and worked in many fields before becoming a writer and wildlife photographer. She lives in Warman, Saskatchewan, with three rabbits, three guinea pigs, two chinchillas, and two rats. Her favourite dinosaur is the *Styracosaurus*.

About the Illustrator

Dianna Bonder has always had a passion for drawing and reading as well as a vivid imagination. When she was a child, her mother wrote stories and Dianna would illustrate them. After studying graphic arts and illustration at the University College of the Cariboo in British Columbia Dianna fulfilled her dream and began working as a professional illustrator.

Illustrating *Digging Canadian Dinosaurs* was an opportunity for her to explore a world which existed millions of years ago. Her research allowed her to get to know the *Edmontosaurus* and the *Troodon,* up close and personal. When asked her favourite Canadian dino, Dianna chose the peaceful plant eating duckbilled dinosaurs.

She lives in Maple Ridge, B.C., with her husband, two domestic cats, one Hairless Sphynx Cat, and three dogs.